CW00517757

Snooker Practice
Log Book
Belong To

Cue Name

Cue Specification

Length	
Configuration	
Tip	
Ferrule	
Shaft Wood	
Joint	
Butt Design	
Bumper	
Price	
Feeling	

Ratings ★ ★ ★ ★ ★

Note

_____

_____

_____

_____

_____

Cue Name

Cue Specification

Length	
Configuration	
Tip	
Ferrule	
Shaft Wood	
Joint	
Butt Design	
Bumper	
Price	
Feeling	

Ratings

★ ★ ★ ★ ★

Note

Cue Name

Cue Specification

Length	
Configuration	
Tip	
Ferrule	
Shaft Wood	
Joint	
Butt Design	
Bumper	
Price	
Feeling	

Ratings ★ ★ ★ ★ ★

Note

Cue Name

Cue Specification

Length	
Configuration	
Tip	
Ferrule	
Shaft Wood	
Joint	
Butt Design	
Bumper	
Price	
Feeling	

Ratings

★ ★ ★ ★ ★

Note

Practice Pattern

Snooker Table Size

Ratings ★ ★ ★ ★ ★

Practice Pattern

Snooker Table Size

Ratings ★ ★ ★ ★ ★

Snooker Table Size

Ratings ★ ★ ★ ★ ★

Snooker Table Size

Ratings ★ ★ ★ ★ ★

Snooker Table Size

Ratings ★ ★ ★ ★ ★

Snooker Table Size

Ratings ★ ★ ★ ★ ★

Snooker Table Size

Ratings ★★★★★

Snooker Table Size

Ratings ★★★★★

Snooker Table Size

Ratings ★ ★ ★ ★ ★

Snooker Table Size

Ratings ★ ★ ★ ★ ★

Practice Pattern

Snooker Table Size

Ratings ★ ★ ★ ★ ★

Practice Pattern

Snooker Table Size

Ratings ★ ★ ★ ★ ★

Snooker Table Size

Ratings ★ ★ ★ ★ ★

Snooker Table Size

Ratings ★ ★ ★ ★ ★

Snooker Table Size

Ratings ★ ★ ★ ★ ★

Snooker Table Size

Ratings ★ ★ ★ ★ ★

Snooker Table Size

Ratings ★ ★ ★ ★ ★

Snooker Table Size

Ratings ★ ★ ★ ★ ★

Snooker Table Size

Ratings ★ ★ ★ ★ ★

Snooker Table Size

Ratings ★ ★ ★ ★ ★

Snooker Table Size

Ratings ★ ★ ★ ★ ★

Snooker Table Size

Ratings ★ ★ ★ ★ ★

Snooker Table Size

Ratings ★ ★ ★ ★ ★

Snooker Table Size

Ratings ★ ★ ★ ★ ★

Snooker Table Size

Ratings ★ ★ ★ ★ ★

Snooker Table Size

Ratings ★ ★ ★ ★ ★

Snooker Table Size

Ratings ★ ★ ★ ★ ★

Practice Pattern

Snooker Table Size

Ratings ★ ★ ★ ★ ★

Practice Pattern

Snooker Table Size

Ratings ★ ★ ★ ★ ★

Practice Pattern

Snooker Table Size

Ratings ★ ★ ★ ★ ★

Snooker Table Size

Ratings

⭐ ⭐ ⭐ ⭐ ⭐

Snooker Table Size

Ratings

⭐ ⭐ ⭐ ⭐ ⭐

Snooker Table Size

Ratings ★ ★ ★ ★ ★

Snooker Table Size

Ratings ★ ★ ★ ★ ★

Snooker Table Size

Ratings ★ ★ ★ ★ ★

Snooker Table Size

Ratings ★ ★ ★ ★ ★

Snooker Table Size

Ratings ★ ★ ★ ★ ★

Snooker Table Size

Ratings ★ ★ ★ ★ ★

Snooker Table Size

Ratings ★ ★ ★ ★ ★

Snooker Table Size

Ratings ★ ★ ★ ★ ★

Snooker Table Size

Ratings ★ ★ ★ ★ ★

Snooker Table Size

Ratings ★ ★ ★ ★ ★

Snooker Table Size

Ratings ★ ★ ★ ★ ★

Snooker Table Size

Ratings ★ ★ ★ ★ ★

Snooker Table Size

Ratings ★ ★ ★ ★ ★

Snooker Table Size

Ratings ★ ★ ★ ★ ★

Snooker Table Size

Ratings ★ ★ ★ ★ ★

Snooker Table Size

Ratings ★ ★ ★ ★ ★

Snooker Table Size

Ratings ★ ★ ★ ★ ★

Snooker Table Size

Ratings ★ ★ ★ ★ ★

Snooker Table Size

Ratings ★ ★ ★ ★ ★

Snooker Table Size

Ratings ★ ★ ★ ★ ★

Snooker Table Size

Ratings ★ ★ ★ ★ ★

Snooker Table Size

Ratings ★ ★ ★ ★ ★

Snooker Table Size

Ratings ★ ★ ★ ★ ★

Snooker Table Size

Ratings ★ ★ ★ ★ ★

Snooker Table Size

Ratings ★ ★ ★ ★ ★

Snooker Table Size

Ratings ★ ★ ★ ★ ★

Practice Pattern

Snooker Table Size

Ratings ★ ★ ★ ★ ★

Practice Pattern

Snooker Table Size

Ratings ★ ★ ★ ★ ★

Snooker Table Size

Ratings ★ ★ ★ ★ ★

Snooker Table Size

Ratings ★ ★ ★ ★ ★

Snooker Table Size

Ratings ★ ★ ★ ★ ★

Snooker Table Size

Ratings ★ ★ ★ ★ ★

Snooker Table Size

Ratings ★ ★ ★ ★ ★

Snooker Table Size

Ratings ★ ★ ★ ★ ★

Snooker Table Size

Ratings ★ ★ ★ ★ ★

Snooker Table Size

Ratings ★ ★ ★ ★ ★

Snooker Table Size

Ratings ★ ★ ★ ★ ★

Snooker Table Size

Ratings ★ ★ ★ ★ ★

Snooker Table Size

Ratings ★ ★ ★ ★ ★

Snooker Table Size

Ratings ★ ★ ★ ★ ★

Snooker Table Size

Ratings ★ ★ ★ ★ ★

Snooker Table Size

Ratings ★ ★ ★ ★ ★

Snooker Table Size

Ratings ★ ★ ★ ★ ★

Practice Pattern

Snooker Table Size

Ratings ★ ★ ★ ★ ★

Snooker Table Size

Ratings ★ ★ ★ ★ ★

Snooker Table Size

Ratings ★ ★ ★ ★ ★

Snooker Table Size

Ratings ★ ★ ★ ★ ★

Snooker Table Size

Ratings ★ ★ ★ ★ ★

Snooker Table Size

Ratings ★ ★ ★ ★ ★

Snooker Table Size

Ratings ★ ★ ★ ★ ★

Snooker Table Size

Ratings ★ ★ ★ ★ ★

Snooker Table Size

Ratings ★ ★ ★ ★ ★

Snooker Table Size

Ratings

★ ★ ★ ★ ★

Snooker Table Size

Ratings

★ ★ ★ ★ ★

Snooker Table Size

Ratings ★ ★ ★ ★ ★

Snooker Table Size

Ratings ★ ★ ★ ★ ★

Practice Pattern

Snooker Table Size

Ratings ★ ★ ★ ★ ★

Practice Pattern

Snooker Table Size

Ratings ★ ★ ★ ★ ★

Snooker Table Size

Ratings ★ ★ ★ ★ ★

Snooker Table Size

Ratings ★ ★ ★ ★ ★

Practice Pattern

Snooker Table Size

Ratings ★ ★ ★ ★ ★

Practice Pattern

Snooker Table Size

Ratings ★ ★ ★ ★ ★

Snooker Table Size

Ratings ★ ★ ★ ★ ★

Snooker Table Size

Ratings ★ ★ ★ ★ ★

Snooker Table Size

Ratings ⭐ ⭐ ⭐ ⭐ ⭐

Snooker Table Size

Ratings ⭐ ⭐ ⭐ ⭐ ⭐

Snooker Table Size

Ratings ★ ★ ★ ★ ★

Snooker Table Size

Ratings ★ ★ ★ ★ ★

Snooker Table Size

Ratings ★ ★ ★ ★ ★

Snooker Table Size

Ratings ★ ★ ★ ★ ★

Snooker Table Size

Ratings ★ ★ ★ ★ ★

Snooker Table Size

Ratings ★ ★ ★ ★ ★

Snooker Table Size

Ratings ⭐⭐⭐⭐⭐

Snooker Table Size

Ratings ⭐⭐⭐⭐⭐

Snooker Table Size

Ratings ★ ★ ★ ★ ★

Snooker Table Size

Ratings ★ ★ ★ ★ ★

Snooker Table Size

Ratings ★ ★ ★ ★ ★

Snooker Table Size

Ratings ★ ★ ★ ★ ★

Snooker Table Size

Ratings ★ ★ ★ ★ ★

Snooker Table Size

Ratings ★ ★ ★ ★ ★

Snooker Table Size

Ratings ★ ★ ★ ★ ★

Snooker Table Size

Ratings ★ ★ ★ ★ ★

Snooker Table Size

Ratings ★ ★ ★ ★ ★

Snooker Table Size

Ratings ★ ★ ★ ★ ★

Snooker Table Size

Ratings ★ ★ ★ ★ ★

Snooker Table Size

Ratings ★ ★ ★ ★ ★

Snooker Table Size

Ratings ★ ★ ★ ★ ★

Snooker Table Size

Ratings ★ ★ ★ ★ ★

Practice Name

Cue Name

Snooker Table Size

Game Practice

Frame	1	2	3	4	5	6	7
Win / Lose							
High Break							
Point							
Snooker							
Escape Form Snooker							
Fouls							
Difficult Shot							
Fluke Shot							

Ratings ★ ★ ★ ★ ★

Note

Practice Name

Cue Name

Snooker Table Size

Game Practice

Frame	1	2	3	4	5	6	7
Win / Lose							
High Break							
Point							
Snooker							
Escape Form Snooker							
Fouls							
Difficult Shot							
Fluke Shot							

Ratings ★ ★ ★ ★ ★

Note

Practice Name

Cue Name

Snooker Table Size

Game Practice

Frame	1	2	3	4	5	6	7
Win / Lose							
High Break							
Point							
Snooker							
Escape Form Snooker							
Fouls							
Difficult Shot							
Fluke Shot							

Ratings ★ ★ ★ ★ ★

Note

Practice Name

Cue Name

Snooker Table Size

Game Practice

Frame	1	2	3	4	5	6	7
Win / Lose							
High Break							
Point							
Snooker							
Escape Form Snooker							
Fouls							
Difficult Shot							
Fluke Shot							

Ratings ★ ★ ★ ★ ★

Note

Practice Name

Cue Name

Snooker Table Size

Game Practice

Frame	1	2	3	4	5	6	7
Win / Lose							
High Break							
Point							
Snooker							
Escape Form Snooker							
Fouls							
Difficult Shot							
Fluke Shot							

Ratings ★ ★ ★ ★ ★

Note

Practice Name

Cue Name

Snooker Table Size

Game Practice

Frame	1	2	3	4	5	6	7
Win / Lose							
High Break							
Point							
Snooker							
Escape Form Snooker							
Fouls							
Difficult Shot							
Fluke Shot							

Ratings ★ ★ ★ ★ ★

Note

Practice Name

Cue Name

Snooker Table Size

Game Practice

Frame	1	2	3	4	5	6	7
Win / Lose							
High Break							
Point							
Snooker							
Escape Form Snooker							
Fouls							
Difficult Shot							
Fluke Shot							

Ratings ★ ★ ★ ★ ★

Note

Practice Name

Cue Name

Snooker Table Size

Game Practice

Frame	1	2	3	4	5	6	7
Win / Lose							
High Break							
Point							
Snooker							
Escape Form Snooker							
Fouls							
Difficult Shot							
Fluke Shot							

Ratings ★ ★ ★ ★ ★

Note

_____

_____

_____

_____

_____

Practice Name

Cue Name

Snooker Table Size

Game Practice

Frame	1	2	3	4	5	6	7
Win / Lose							
High Break							
Point							
Snooker							
Escape Form Snooker							
Fouls							
Difficult Shot							
Fluke Shot							

Ratings ★ ★ ★ ★ ★

Note

Practice Name

Cue Name

Snooker Table Size

Game Practice

Frame	1	2	3	4	5	6	7
Win / Lose							
High Break							
Point							
Snooker							
Escape Form Snooker							
Fouls							
Difficult Shot							
Fluke Shot							

Ratings ★ ★ ★ ★ ★

Note

Practice Name

Cue Name

Snooker Table Size

Game Practice

Frame	1	2	3	4	5	6	7
Win / Lose							
High Break							
Point							
Snooker							
Escape Form Snooker							
Fouls							
Difficult Shot							
Fluke Shot							

Ratings

★ ★ ★ ★ ★

Note

_____

_____

_____

_____

_____

Practice Name

Cue Name

Snooker Table Size

Game Practice

Frame	1	2	3	4	5	6	7
Win / Lose							
High Break							
Point							
Snooker							
Escape Form Snooker							
Fouls							
Difficult Shot							
Fluke Shot							

Ratings ★ ★ ★ ★ ★

Note

Practice Name

Cue Name

Snooker Table Size

Game Practice

Frame	1	2	3	4	5	6	7
Win / Lose							
High Break							
Point							
Snooker							
Escape Form Snooker							
Fouls							
Difficult Shot							
Fluke Shot							

Ratings ★ ★ ★ ★ ★

Note

Practice Name

Cue Name

Snooker Table Size

Game Practice

Frame	1	2	3	4	5	6	7
Win / Lose							
High Break							
Point							
Snooker							
Escape Form Snooker							
Fouls							
Difficult Shot							
Fluke Shot							

Ratings ★ ★ ★ ★ ★

Note

Practice Name

Cue Name

Snooker Table Size

Game Practice

Frame	1	2	3	4	5	6	7
Win / Lose							
High Break							
Point							
Snooker							
Escape Form Snooker							
Fouls							
Difficult Shot							
Fluke Shot							

Ratings ★ ★ ★ ★ ★

Note

Practice Name

Cue Name

Snooker Table Size

Game Practice

Frame	1	2	3	4	5	6	7
Win / Lose							
High Break							
Point							
Snooker							
Escape Form Snooker							
Fouls							
Difficult Shot							
Fluke Shot							

Ratings ★ ★ ★ ★ ★

Note

Practice Name

Cue Name

Snooker Table Size

Game Practice

Frame	1	2	3	4	5	6	7
Win / Lose							
High Break							
Point							
Snooker							
Escape Form Snooker							
Fouls							
Difficult Shot							
Fluke Shot							

Ratings ★ ★ ★ ★ ★

Note

Practice Name

Cue Name

Snooker Table Size

Game Practice

Frame	1	2	3	4	5	6	7
Win / Lose							
High Break							
Point							
Snooker							
Escape Form Snooker							
Fouls							
Difficult Shot							
Fluke Shot							

Ratings ★ ★ ★ ★ ★

Note

Practice Name

Cue Name

Snooker Table Size

Game Practice

Frame	1	2	3	4	5	6	7
Win / Lose							
High Break							
Point							
Snooker							
Escape Form Snooker							
Fouls							
Difficult Shot							
Fluke Shot							

Ratings ★ ★ ★ ★ ★

Note

Practice Name

Cue Name

Snooker Table Size

Game Practice

Frame	1	2	3	4	5	6	7
Win / Lose							
High Break							
Point							
Snooker							
Escape Form Snooker							
Fouls							
Difficult Shot							
Fluke Shot							

Ratings ★ ★ ★ ★ ★

Note

Practice Name

Cue Name

Snooker Table Size

Game Practice

Frame	1	2	3	4	5	6	7
Win / Lose							
High Break							
Point							
Snooker							
Escape Form Snooker							
Fouls							
Difficult Shot							
Fluke Shot							

Ratings ★ ★ ★ ★ ★

Note

Practice Name

Cue Name

Snooker Table Size

Game Practice

Frame	1	2	3	4	5	6	7
Win / Lose							
High Break							
Point							
Snooker							
Escape Form Snooker							
Fouls							
Difficult Shot							
Fluke Shot							

Ratings ★ ★ ★ ★ ★

Note

Practice Name

Cue Name

Snooker Table Size

Game Practice

Frame	1	2	3	4	5	6	7
Win / Lose							
High Break							
Point							
Snooker							
Escape Form Snooker							
Fouls							
Difficult Shot							
Fluke Shot							

Ratings ★ ★ ★ ★ ★

Note

Practice Name

Cue Name

Snooker Table Size

Game Practice

Frame	1	2	3	4	5	6	7
Win / Lose							
High Break							
Point							
Snooker							
Escape Form Snooker							
Fouls							
Difficult Shot							
Fluke Shot							

Ratings ★ ★ ★ ★ ★

Note

Practice Name

Cue Name

Snooker Table Size

Game Practice

Frame	1	2	3	4	5	6	7
Win / Lose							
High Break							
Point							
Snooker							
Escape Form Snooker							
Fouls							
Difficult Shot							
Fluke Shot							

Ratings ★ ★ ★ ★ ★

Note

Practice Name

Cue Name

Snooker Table Size

Game Practice

Frame	1	2	3	4	5	6	7
Win / Lose							
High Break							
Point							
Snooker							
Escape Form Snooker							
Fouls							
Difficult Shot							
Fluke Shot							

Ratings ★ ★ ★ ★ ★

Note

_____

_____

_____

_____

_____

Practice Name

Cue Name

Snooker Table Size

Game Practice

Frame	1	2	3	4	5	6	7
Win / Lose							
High Break							
Point							
Snooker							
Escape Form Snooker							
Fouls							
Difficult Shot							
Fluke Shot							

Ratings ★ ★ ★ ★ ★

Note

Practice Name

Cue Name

Snooker Table Size

Game Practice

Frame	1	2	3	4	5	6	7
Win / Lose							
High Break							
Point							
Snooker							
Escape Form Snooker							
Fouls							
Difficult Shot							
Fluke Shot							

Ratings ★ ★ ★ ★ ★

Note

Practice Name

Cue Name

Snooker Table Size

Game Practice

Frame	1	2	3	4	5	6	7
Win / Lose							
High Break							
Point							
Snooker							
Escape Form Snooker							
Fouls							
Difficult Shot							
Fluke Shot							

Ratings ★ ★ ★ ★ ★

Note

Practice Name

Cue Name

Snooker Table Size

Game Practice

Frame	1	2	3	4	5	6	7
Win / Lose							
High Break							
Point							
Snooker							
Escape Form Snooker							
Fouls							
Difficult Shot							
Fluke Shot							

Ratings ★ ★ ★ ★ ★

Note

Printed in Great Britain
by Amazon

76731199R00058